'To Fran. Enjoy!

Mrs H

For Mum who encouraged me to write and Dad who made it possible...

www.montaguepublishing.co.uk

Copyright © Jon Bridgeman 2010

Jon Bridgeman has asserted his rights under the
Copyright, Designs and Patents Act, 1988,
To be identified as the author of this work.

All rights reserved.
No part of this publication may be reproduced, stored in a
retrieval system, or transmitted in any form or by any means,
electronic, mechanical, photocopying, recording or otherwise,
without prior permission of the author.

A catalogue of this book
is available from the British Library

ISBN 978-0-9566152-1-3

Illustrations by Rachel Cooper

Printed and bound in the UK by Cambridge Print Solutions, 1 Ronald Rolph Court, Wadloes Road, Cambridge, CB58PX

First published in the UK in 2010 by

www.montaguepublishing.co.uk

JON BRIDGEMAN
Tommy Tomkins and the Snowdog

Illustrated by Rachel Cooper

Contents

1. It's snow joke!   7
2. An amazing discovery   18
3. Billy has a plan   26
4. Feeling hot, hot, hot.   38
5. We're toast!   52
6. Snow-Dog's too cool.   64

1. It's snow joke!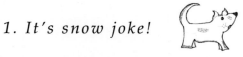

Small, puffy, white balls of snow landed softly on the window sill of Number 31 Broad Lake Avenue. Thomas Tomkins looked out of the window miserably, as he watched other children running around in the meadow throwing snowballs and building snowmen. Thomas, or Tommy as he liked to be called, was not like most nine year old boys. Yes, he had posters of his favourite football team Chelsea plastered to his wall. Yes, he thought the best thing about school was when the bell went for home time. Yes, he couldn't understand why girls would skip in the playground when they could be kicking a football. But there was one thing about Tommy that was different to most nine year old boys. Tommy didn't like snow...in fact he hated it!

Two weeks ago Mr. Jeffries, Tommy's teacher, had spoken to Class 3J. He'd shuffled the papers on his messy desk, fiddled with his silly white moustache and cleared his throat in his very annoying manner.
"Huhh huh hurrrr," he coughed. "The Christmas holidays are really going to be fun this year," he'd said.
Tommy looked over at his friend Billy, who was holding a small ruler under his nose and pretending it was a moustache

like Mr. Jeffries'. Tommy and Billy called Mr. Jeffries 'Walrus-face' behind his back.

"Excuse me Mr. Jeffries sir but why will it be such a good Christmas?" asked Suzie Nicholls, Mr. Jeffries' favourite pupil. Suzie sat in the front row and annoyed Tommy by always sticking her hand in the air and her hair in her mouth. Mr. Jeffries continued.
"This year it's going to snow. It said so on the television this morning. It's going to be a white Christmas!" he announced. Suzie Nicholls looked like she might actually burst with excitement and all the other children had cheered and screamed, all that is apart from Tommy and his best friend Billy. Snow to Tommy and Billy meant only one thing... no football. No football to Tommy and Billy was a fate worse than death. Well, certainly worse than one of Mr. Jeffries' boring mathematics lessons anyway!

Tommy remembered the bell sounding for the end of school and all his class running out of school into the

playground. Everyone was smiling and staring up at the sky as Mr. Jeffries' prediction had come true. Snow was already starting to fall from the sky. Some of the children were sticking out their tongues trying to catch the snow. Even Mr. Jeffries looked unusually happy as snow fell on his head, making him look more like a walrus than ever.
"Have a wonderful Christmas Suzie," the teacher smiled. "And don't forget that extra maths homework!"
"I won't sir!" Suzie beamed.
Mr. Jeffries hurried past Tommy to his beaten up old Ford Fiesta car.
"You too Jenkins!" Mr. Jeffries mumbled.
"Tomkins sir," Tommy replied but Mr. Jeffries was already gone and moving across the playground faster than Tommy had ever seen him move.
"Walrus-face is in a rush. Hey, you think teachers like school holidays as much as us?" asked Billy.
"Maybe more than us!" replied Tommy as Mr. Jeffries roared past, his car booming out a rock tune the boys had never heard before.

Tommy and Billy had trudged home with their hands deep in their pockets.
"You know what happens if it keeps snowing?" asked Billy.
"Yeah, I know and don't even say it. If you say it, it's bound to happen!" replied Tommy.
"Well, if it snows for two weeks we can't play football," said Billy sadly.
"I told you not to say it!" snapped Tommy.
"Sorry Tommy," mumbled Billy, even more miserably.
 "Look, don't worry Bill. Maybe it won't snow all holiday and then we can play football," said Tommy trying to cheer him up.
"Alright Tommy. Look, I'll see you tomorrow, maybe the snow will be all gone then," smiled Billy running off across the meadow.

But Billy could not have been more wrong. It had snowed almost every day of the holidays. It was like a white blanket had covered the meadow, making it impossible to play football there. Now, as he stared out the window, Tommy knew that there were only six days of their holiday left and their chances of playing football looked really slim. If he had to go back to lessons with Walrus-face without playing football, it would be officially the worst thing that had ever happened to him. He stared out of the window at the fresh snow.

He stared up at the heavy looking clouds. "Will you stop it now!" he said to the clouds. "Haven't we had enough snow?"

Tommy left the window and slumped down on his bed. He picked up his brand new football that he'd got for Christmas. He held it up to his fish tank.
"What's wrong with this?" he asked his goldfish.
The goldfish stared at Tommy through the bowl. Then it swum around the castle for the millionth time that day.
"I'll tell you what's wrong with it, it's too clean that's what," huffed Tommy at the fish.
"A football needs to be used,"
Tommy picked up the ball, threw it against the wall and headed it when it bounced back. Then he did it again, and again, and again, and again until....
"Tommy!" shouted his mother. "Stop bouncing that ball and go out and play!"
"Don't want to, it's snowing," replied Tommy moodily.
"Well, if you don't stop bouncing that ball in the house I'll let all the air out of it. Anyway, I've just come in and I'm

sure it stopped snowing a moment ago," said Mum.

"Really Mum?' said Tommy, jumping downstairs two at a time to meet his mother in the kitchen.

"Yes really!" said Mum. "I've just walked in and look, can you see any white snow in my hair?"

"No mum, I can't," said Tommy laughing. "I can only see white hair! Just joking Mum and I'm going to Billy's and I won't be late, and I'll be careful and bye!" said Tommy quickly.

"Umm, err, ok," replied his confused mum. "I'll never understand ten year old boys," she muttered.

 Tommy bolted out of the door and raced across the meadow to Billy's house. As he ran, he could see his mum had been right, it had stopped snowing. Now, if it would just melt, they could play football. Tommy ran up the drive skidding a bit on the snow. He knocked on the door and panted breathlessly. Billy's mum answered the door.

 "Hello Tommy, how are you?" she said.

"Great Mrs. Todd, I'm great thank you and it's stopped snowing so I'm really great. Is Billy here?" replied Tommy.
"Yes, he's upstairs sulking, he'll be pleased to see you though," smiled Billy's mum.
Billy's mum shouted upstairs and in a flash, Billy came bounding down the stairs. As always he was wearing his favourite Chelsea football shirt with his name 'Todd' and number 9 across the back.
"Billy it's stopped snowing!" said Tommy excitedly.
"Yessssss!" cheered Billy, down on his knees doing a very good impression of a Premiership footballer scoring a goal.
"Can we play now?"
"Not yet Billy, it has to melt first...but maybe tomorrow?" Tommy smiled.
"Great! Really great! You wanna play video games upstairs?" asked Billy.
"Yeah, alright. How about your Golden Goals?"
"I wouldn't have suggested anything else!" laughed Billy with a huge grin.

2. An amazing discovery

The next day Tommy woke up really early and he was even more excited than he had been on Christmas morning. He rushed to the window and pulled back the curtains. There was already bright sunshine, just like there had been all day yesterday, but better than that, Tommy could see grass. Green grass! The meadow was still covered in patches of snow, but it was mainly green again.
"Yes!" shouted Tommy. "No more snow, no more snowmen and no more snowballs. It's footballs from now on!"
He got dressed in record time and wolfed down his breakfast.
"Why are you in such a hurry?" his mum asked.
"P-p-laying f-football," Tommy spluttered, with cornflakes still in his mouth.
"Tommy, eat slower you'll get indigestion."

"Finished now mum," Tommy smiled, rinsing his bowl in the sink.
"Dishwasher. It takes two seconds to put it in the dishwasher, sometimes even your father manages that," tutted mum.
   "What do I manage dear?" asked Tommy's father walking into the kitchen with his head buried in the sport section of the newspaper and put his empty bowl in the sink.
"Oh never mind, you boys are as bad as one another," muttered mum.
"Bye Tommy!" shouted Dad. "The Blues are on TV tonight."
"Great dad, who we got?" replied Tommy rushing back into the kitchen.
"Playing West Ham tonight," said Dad, as he kissed Tommy's mum and grabbed a piece of toast.
"Have a good day!" dad shouted as he slammed the door. Tommy grabbed his new football and rushed out of the house.
"Your coat!" his mum shouted.
"Don't need it...not cold!" shouted Tommy as the door slammed behind him. As mum shook her head Tommy appeared again and grabbed his coat.

"Thought you weren't cold and you didn't need it?" asked mum.
"I'm not but we need goalposts...bye Mum!" The door slammed again.
"I don't understand boys... or men," said mum, finally sitting down to drink her tea.

When Tommy got to Billy's house his best mate was already waiting for him. They said goodbye to Billy's mum and rushed out to the meadow. The grass was

still a little damp but they put down their coats and began playing. Billy started in goal and Tommy took shots. As usual, Billy carried out a running commentary of the game just as if they were on TV. Billy started.
"And here comes Tomkins, he beats one man, slips past the defender, he's having a great game today, surely the England manager is watching in the stands, is he going to pull the trigger...he shoots......he scores!!!"
Tommy did score. He shot the ball straight past Billy and into the trees at the back of the meadow.
"Oh no! My new ball's gone in the trees, it better not be burst," said Tommy crossly.
"And Tomkins is going to the crowd, what a celebration!" continued Billy, still commentating.
"Yeah yeah," said Tommy as he went to fetch the ball.

Tommy walked behind their goal and into the trees. The trees still had a little bit of snow on them. Tommy saw his ball

and picked it up, brushing mud and twigs off it. It didn't look burst.
"It's OK, I've got it and it's not burst!" he shouted back to Billy. He started to go back to the meadow when he heard something very strange. It sounded like someone crying.
"Umm...hello. Is anyone there?" asked Tommy.
He heard a crying noise again. Tommy looked around. He couldn't see anyone. There were only a few trees and what looked like a snowman that someone had made in the shape of a dog. Tommy listened again. The crying sound seemed to be coming from the tree near the snowman shaped like a dog. Tommy moved closer. It couldn't be? He listened carefully. Yes, he was certain. The crying was coming from the snow-dog.

"Excuse me, are you crying?" Tommy said feeling a little silly. What was he doing talking to snow?
The crying sound stopped. I must be imagining it Tommy said to himself, smiling and shaking his head. He'd obviously headed the football too much.

He started to turn to go back to the meadow.

"Help me!"

Tommy spun round, looking at the snow-dog.

"Help me!"

The sound had definitely come from the snow-dog. Tommy bent down and inspected it. It was a small dog made out of snow, with a potato cut in half for its ears, marbles for eyes, a stone nose, an orange peel for a mouth, twigs for whiskers and a carrot for a tail. Whoever had built it had done a really good job; it was a very good snow-dog.

"Umm...did you say something?" asked Tommy, feeling foolish again.
"Yes I did," said the snow-dog. "I said help me!"
"Oh....er...that's what I thought you said," replied Tommy looking very confused.
"Well can you...help me?" asked the snow-dog.
"Umm...yes...of course I can. It's just I'm a little surprised. I didn't think snowmen, I mean snow-dogs, could talk!"
"Oh sorry," said the snow-dog sadly.

"No it's OK," said Tommy feeling very sorry for the poor little thing. "How can I help?"
"I want to melt!" said the snow-dog.
"Oh!" replied Tommy, still in shock.

The little snow-dog told Tommy that someone had built a whole snow family two weeks ago. There had been a snow-dad, a snow-mum, snow-children and a snow-dog. But then they had all melted and now the snow-dog was very sad and all on his own.
"Oh look, don't worry!" said Tommy. "All snowmen melt eventually."
"Really?" asked the snow-dog.
"Of course," laughed Tommy. "I'll just go and get my friend and we'll move you into the meadow in the sun and you'll melt in no time!"
"Oh, thank you ever so much!" said the snow-dog happily.
Tommy rushed back to the meadow and told Billy his incredible story. At first Billy didn't believe him, but when Tommy took him to see the snow-dog he realized Tommy had been telling the truth. Recovering from his shock, Billy

rushed back to his house and grabbed his sled and brought it back to the meadow. Tommy and Billy carefully put the snow-dog on the sled and pulled him into the meadow in the sunlight. The snow-dog was really happy and thanked the two boys. The boys were disappointed but they had to go home. They said goodbye to the snow-dog and ran off.

"Tommy, that was cool. A talking snow-dog!" laughed Billy as they rushed across the meadow.
"Yeah, that was cool. I even forgot about playing football," giggled Tommy.
"Do you think he'll melt?" asked Billy.
"Of course he will. Snowmen always melt!" said Tommy.

3. Billy has a plan

Tommy woke up even more excited than the day before, but this time he wasn't thinking about football. He wanted to see if the snow-dog was still there. Had the snow-dog melted? Tommy hurriedly pulled on some clothes and bounded downstairs. He grabbed the cereal box from the cupboard and poured it into a bowl. Tommy then spooned the cereal into his mouth as quick as he could.
"Tommy, what are you doing?" asked Tommy's mum.
"Eating cereal mum,' replied Tommy finishing his bowl.
"Without milk?" asked his mum puzzled.
"Yeah it's quicker that way!" said Tommy.
"You can't eat cereal without milk!" said mum.
"Oh ok," answered Tommy.
He went to the fridge, poured himself a glass of milk and drank it.
"There you go, mum. Cereal and milk!" Tommy smiled as he raced towards the door.

"Well, that's the funniest way of eating cereal I've ever seen!" said mum. "I'll never understand ten year old boys!"

Tommy ran across the meadow as fast as he could. Billy was already there and to Tommy's surprise, so was the snow-dog...it hadn't melted at all.
"He's still here!" exclaimed Tommy.
"Yeah and he's still crying," said Billy bending down next to the snow-dog. Tommy knelt down too.
"It's been really sunny and I still haven't melted," sobbed snow-dog.
"Hey, don't cry. We'll help you," said Billy.
"Yeah we will," said Tommy. "Umm, Billy could I have a quick word over here?" asked Tommy, pointing for Billy to join him away from the snow-dog. When they were far enough away that the snow-dog couldn't hear them Tommy continued.
"Look I agree that we should help it, but how exactly are we going to do that?" asked Tommy.
"Don't worry. I've got a plan!" Billy grinned.

"Look no offence Billy, but sometimes your ideas aren't that great!" said Tommy.
"What do you mean?" Billy frowned.
"Well, there was that time that you told our teacher Mr. Jeffries that we should go on a trip to France to see the Awful Tower!" replied Tommy.
"Yeah what's wrong with that, we were studying France?" huffed Billy.

"Yes Billy, but it's the Eiffel tower not the Awful Tower!" shrugged Tommy.

"Yeah, well it was still a good idea and anyway have you got an idea?" asked Billy grumpily.
"No not at the moment," answered Tommy.
"Well here's mine," said Billy.
Billy whispered his idea into Tommy's ear. When he was finished Tommy looked at him and said:
"You know what Billy, that could just work!"

    They put the snow-dog on the sled and headed toward Billy's house. Although all of the snow had melted, they could still easily drag snow-dog on the sled. When they got to the house they went round to the back door.
"Right, keep quiet," whispered Billy. "I don't think mum would be too happy with me bringing the snow-dog into the house."
Very quietly the two boys opened the door and crept in. They gently lifted the snow-dog into the kitchen and put him down next to the radiator. Billy explained the plan to the snow-dog.

"Right, this is a radiator. It gets very hot and heats up the whole house. It's got very hot water inside it. If we leave you next to this radiator you're bound to melt."
"Fantastic!" said the snow-dog happily. "Then I'll be just like all my friends."
Billy bent down and turned up the radiator to its very hottest. Tommy pulled over a couple of chairs.
"Is your mum in?" asked Tommy.
"No I don't think so, she'd have probably heard us by now," smiled Billy.

The two friends sat and watched the snow-dog. They looked at the snow-dog. Then they looked at the kitchen clock. They looked at the snow-dog. Then they looked at the kitchen clock. Snow-dog...clock. Snow dog...clock. Snow dog...clock until.....

"Umm, Billy that's been nearly an hour now!" said Tommy.
"Yeah you're right. It's not hot enough. I know I'll just get something, I'll be back in a minute," said Billy rushing off upstairs.
Tommy looked at the poor little snow-dog. It was starting to get very sad again.
"What's wrong with me?" asked the snow-dog. "Why can't I melt and be with my friends?"
"Don't be sad. We'll find a way to help you, I promise" said Tommy, patting the snow-dog's cold little head.
Tommy heard a thumping noise as Billy jumped down the stairs two at a time.
"Got it!" shouted Billy.
"Got what?" asked Tommy.
"This!" said Billy as he burst back into the kitchen.

Billy was holding a very large hairdryer. It was big and black with lots of buttons. It looked very expensive.

"It's my mum's. She got it for Christmas. It's really powerful and gets really hot," smiled Billy.

Billy plugged it in, turned it to full power and pointed it at snow-dog.

"This'll do the trick!" shouted Billy over the noise of the hairdryer.

"I hope so!" Tommy shouted back to him. While their great plan was in action Tommy and Billy couldn't hear anything over the noise of the powerful hairdryer. If they'd have been able to hear they would have heard the sound of a car pulling into Billy's drive. Billy's mum had been to the supermarket in town, but now she was back carrying a lot of shopping bags. If they'd been able to hear they would have heard the car door slam and the noise of high heels clicking on the concrete driveway. If they'd have been able to hear they would have heard the front door open and close. If they'd been able to hear they may have heard Billy's mum walk into the kitchen and drop her shopping bags at the shock of

what she saw. But of course, they couldn't hear...well not until Billy's mum screamed out loud.
"Arrrgghhhhhhhhhhhhhhhhhhhh!!!!!!!!!!
!!!!!!!!!!!"

At the sound of his mum screaming poor Billy dropped the hairdryer, making it pull its plug out of the wall. Billy and Tommy turned around and stared at a very, very angry looking mum. It looked as though steam was coming out of her ears.
"Billy Todd! Just what on earth are you doing in my kitchen with my brand new hairdryer?" said Billy's mum angrily.
"Umm....I'm....er.....trying to melt this snow-dog," replied Billy sheepishly.
"What do you mean you're trying to melt a snow-dog?" she shouted at him.
"Well we found this snow-dog in the meadow and we wanted to melt him so I thought we could melt him with the radiator but that wasn't working so...."
Billy never got to finish his story. His mum interrupted him!
"Out!" she shouted at Billy and Tommy.
"But mum..." said Billy

"Out!" she shouted again.
"But what about?"
"OUT!!!!!" she screamed.
The two boys didn't need to be told again. They picked up the snow-dog and bolted out of the back door as fast as they could. Billy's mum was still shouting at them as they ran back towards the meadow.
"And if my hairdryer's broken Billy Todd then there'll be no pocket money for a month, no make that a year, no, make it never!"

When they got back to the meadow they sat down exhausted. The little snow-dog hadn't melted at all. Tommy spoke first.
"Well I guess that didn't work."
"No, guess not," replied Billy.
"Sorry about the pocket money," said Tommy.
"Don't worry, it might not be broken," shrugged Billy.

"I've never seen your mum look so angry," said Tommy.
"Yeah I thought she was going to explode," replied Billy.
The two boys looked at each other and then burst into laughter. They laughed until they cried at the thought of Mrs. Todd exploding like a volcano. Finally they stopped laughing and both looked at snow-dog. The poor little thing still looked really sad.
"Don't worry little snow-dog, we'll think of something," smiled Tommy kindly.
"Yes we will," said Billy. "In fact I've thought of something already!"
"Oh no Billy, not again!" said Tommy.
"Don't worry Tom. This one's a much better idea. We'll definitely melt him tomorrow. Now I better go and see if mum's cooled down a bit. Hope that hairdryer's not broken!"
And with a wink and a wave Billy ran off, leaving Tommy with the snow-dog.

Tommy sat down next to their new little friend.

"Do you think he'll have a better plan tomorrow?" asked the snow-dog hopefully.

"I don't know, but we will find a way to help you, I promise," said Tommy

"Thank you, you're both being really kind to me," said snow dog, his marble eyes looking happily at Tommy.

Tommy patted him on the head and then stood up to leave.

"No problem. Look I've got to go now. We'll see you tomorrow snow-dog. At least Billy's idea can't be any worse than today's!"

4. Feeling hot, hot, hot.

Tommy bounced out of bed and looked out of the window. It was a beautiful sunny day again. He wondered if the snow-dog had melted overnight. Tommy looked at his calendar on his bedroom wall. He crossed off another day and realised that there was only a few days now until they went back to school. He hoped that they'd solve the snow dog problem before then. He bounced down the stairs again and sat down at the breakfast table, pouring himself a bowl of his favourite cereal. This time he added milk and began eating quickly.
"Hey, slow down Tommy. There's plenty of time to play football. Take your time with your food!" said Tommy's mum.
"Yeah, OK mum," replied Tommy, barely slowing down at all.
"Honestly, you'll get indigestion!" mum tutted.
Tommy finished his cereal, gulped a glass of orange juice and went over and kissed his mum goodbye. Then he was

out the door and racing across the meadow.
"That boy really is crazy about football," smiled mum to herself.
She bent down to put a tea-bag in the bin and saw Tommy's football on the floor. She quickly opened the window and shouted after him.
"Tommy, Tommy, you've forgotten your football!"
But Tommy was already too far away across the meadow to hear her.
"That's funny. He never forgets his football. I'll never understand ten year old boys!" she smiled to herself.

On the other side of the meadow, Billy was in a hurry too. Luckily for him he hadn't broken his mum's hairdryer. He'd escaped with a big telling off about not touching things that belonged to his mum. So with his pocket money safe he was keen to try out his next idea. He raced out of the door and across the meadow. Tommy had beaten him this morning and he was already standing next to the snow-dog.

"He's still really lonely," said Tommy pointing to the snow-dog.
'Yeah, he looks so sad," said Billy bending down to pat the snow-dog's head.
"All my friends have gone and I want to go too," said the snow-dog sadly.
"Don't worry. I've got an idea!" grinned Billy.
"I hope it's better than last time," sighed Tommy.
"It is. We need more heat and I know where to get it!" smiled Billy.
"Where?" asked Tommy, suspicious of his best friend's idea.
"I've brought my skateboard. Let's put the snow-dog on it," said Billy.
The two boys lifted snow-dog and gently put him on Billy's skateboard.
"Where are we going?" asked the snow-dog.
"We're going into town," replied Billy.
Tommy put his coat over the snow-dog so that nobody asked any stupid questions and the boys pushed him into town. They walked past the school, the newsagents and the hairdressers and then Billy stopped outside the post-office.

"What are we doing…posting him to Africa?" asked Tommy,
"No we're going over there, to my Aunty Judy's place!" replied Billy.
Realisation suddenly dawned on Tommy's face as he looked at Aunty Judy's place.
"Oh! Look I think I know the idea Billy, but won't we get in trouble?" asked Tommy.
"No. My Aunty Judy won't mind and anyway she's not in this morning, she's doing mum's nails!" replied Billy.

Billy's Aunty Judy owned 'Altering Images', a Beauty Salon in town. The salon did hair, make-up, nails and one other thing. The salon was also a Tanning shop and it had two big machines that people stood in and got an all over tan without ever having to go on holiday.

It was the tanning machines that interested Billy. His mum had once told him how hot the machines got inside them and when Tommy had mentioned heat, Billy had thought of the sun beds. Maybe they were hot enough to melt a snow-dog!
Billy explained the plan.
"Right Tommy, I'll distract Sandra the girl at the counter and you get the snow-dog inside the tanning machine."

Billy went through the door. A girl with almost orange skin and bright

blonde hair sat behind the counter, filing her nails. She was watching a small TV behind the counter, which was loudly blaring out the noise of a daytime soap opera.
"Welcome to Altering Images, how can I help you?" she said without even looking up.
"Hey Sandra, it's me Billy," smiled Billy looking up at her orange face.
"Oh...it's you," Sandra said a little distastefully, briefly looking up from filing her claw-like nails. "Whadda you want?"

"Aunty Judy sent me to ask you for a box of nail polish," said Billy.

"Oh…I'll have to get it from the stockroom," said Sandra.
"OK thanks" smiled Billy.
"From the stockroom? All the way in the back? Can't she wait?" Sandra asked, reluctant to leave her soap opera and important nail filing.
"No, she needs it now, she's doing my mum's nails. I'll wait for you here," replied Billy.
"Oh for goodness sake honestly, can't you see I'm busy?"
"Yeah, you look rushed off your feet," Billy grinned.
Sandra got up, staring daggers at Billy, and put her nail file down. Blowing her finger nails and still giving Billy evil eyes she tottered into the back on huge white stilettos.

As soon as Sandra's back was turned Billy gave Tommy the thumbs up signal. Tommy picked up the snow-dog and carried him into the shop and through the Tanning room door. Billy followed him in and closed the door behind him. Sandra returned with the box of nail polish.

"Oh...where's he gone then? Silly boy!" she said
Sandra sat down and went back to filing her nails and watching TV.
"Ooh that Ricardo's ever so handsome!" she said to no-one in particular.

Inside the Tanning room Billy winked at Tommy and handed him a small pair of black goggles.
"What are these for? Are we going swimming?" asked Tommy.
"No, they protect your eyes," replied Billy.
They opened the door of the tanning machine and lifted the snow-dog inside, closing the door behind them.
"This should do it," smiled Billy.
He turned the Tanning machine to high and set the timer for 20 minutes and then they sat down and waited. After 2 minutes they were feeling a little hot. After 5 minutes they were starting to sweat. After 10 minutes they were very hot and covered in sweat. After 12 minutes they could barely stand the heat any longer, but the snow-dog hadn't melted one little drop.

"It's no good Billy, it's not working!" said Tommy.
"You're right the snow-dog hasn't melted at all!" agreed Billy.
"If we don't get out of here soon we're going to melt!" said Tommy.
"Just give it 5 more minutes," pleaded Billy.
Tommy agreed with him and they waited. After 15 minutes their goggles had steamed up so they couldn't see. After 17 minutes their clothes were wet with sweat. The inside of the tanning room was filled with steam and Tommy couldn't even see Billy who was just in front of him. After 19 minutes the door opened!
"Brilliant it's finished!" shouted Tommy.
"No, I didn't hear the beep," replied Billy.
"But the door opened!" said Tommy.
"It did?" said Billy.

Billy wiped his fingers over the goggles, clearing the steam away but he wasn't pleased with what he saw. Standing fuming at the door was Aunty Jud,y her bright pink hair glowing in

rage. She reached into the tanning machine and grabbed Billy's ear with her beautifully painted fingernails.
"Billy Todd! What do you think you're doing in my tanning machine?" Aunty Judy asked a wriggling Billy.
"Oww...er...nothing Aunty," replied Billy painfully.
"Doesn't look like nothing to me. Looks like you and your little friend are up to something!" she said crossly. She grabbed Tommy's ear with the other hand and Tommy could feel why Billy had complained. Her nails were really sharp.
"No Aunty, it's just we were trying to melt this snow-dog!"
"Does this look like a microwave to you boys?" Aunty Judy asked.
The boys shook their heads.
"Does this look like an oven to you boys?" Aunty Judy asked.
The boys shook their heads.
"Well then, it's not for cooking or melting things then is it?" Aunty Judy asked.
The two boys miserably shook their heads again.

"Get out Tommy," she snapped and she pulled Tommy and snow-dog out of the tanning machine.
Aunty Judy bent down and inspected her machine.
"Luckily for you two bird brains there's no water on the floor and the machine is fine!" she said.
The two boys breathed a sigh of relief.

But Aunty Judy wasn't finished telling them off.
"Now go on home before I call your mothers and if I ever see you in my shop again...I'll paint your fingernails pink! Go on, get out!" she shouted.
The boys didn't need to be told again. They raced out of the shop and ran all the way home, pulling snow-dog with them.

Aunty Judy stomped back into the reception.
"Sandra!" she shouted.
Sandra quickly came out from behind the counter smoothing her skirt nervously with her hands.
"...and just how did those two boys manage to get past you and get into my tanning machine?" Aunt Judy asked crossly.
"Oh...I er...dunno Miss Brown," Sandra stammered.
"Probably because you were watching that stupid soap opera again!" barked Aunt Judy.
"No...I mean...yes...Mrs. Brown!" replied Sandra getting close to tears.

"First you let poor old Mrs. Higgins go from a luxurious brown to lobster red and now this. Last chance Sandra...last chance!" stormed Aunt Judy swaggering out of the salon.

Sandra watched her boss go and sat down behind the counter and switched off the TV.

"I hate that Billy Todd!" she screamed slamming her nail file down, breaking a nail.

When they reached the meadow they sat down. The plan had failed badly. The little snow-dog hadn't melted a drop and they'd got in trouble again. The two boys looked red and brown in the face as if they'd been sitting in the sun too long. Things weren't going well.

"Ok Billy, no more of your ideas. I'm tired of getting in trouble!" said Tommy.

"Alright, no more ideas," said Billy miserably. "What shall we do then?"

"This snow-dog needs our help and he's going to melt if it's the last thing we do. But this time....I'll come up with an idea!" smiled Tommy.

"Will it be better than mine?" asked Billy.
"Well it couldn't be worse!" laughed Tommy.

5. We're toast!

Tommy sat down at the desk in his room and scribbled down ideas with a pencil. Billy's plan had promise. They did need more heat but where could they get it without getting in trouble? Tommy wrote down a few ideas and then scratched them out. Where was there heat that they could use?
"Tommy," shouted mum from downstairs. "Come and get some toast. Dad's got fresh bread this morning!"
"That's it!" said Tommy. 'I've got it!"
He bolted down the stairs, grabbed a hot slice of toast and ran out of the door.
"Where's he off to in such a hurry?" asked Dad.
"I don't know," sighed Mum. "I'll never understand ten year old boys!"

Tommy got to Billy's house just as they finished breakfast and then the two boys ran to the meadow. The little snow-dog was just where they'd left him and he still hadn't melted a bit. Tommy explained to Billy his idea.

"Basically, you had a good idea. We needed more heat. But everywhere we went we got in trouble. So what we need is a lot of heat, somewhere outside where no-one can tell us off!" said Tommy.
"Sounds good, but where?" asked Billy.
"Go and grab your skateboard and I'll take you there," said Tommy.
Billy dashed back across the meadow and Tommy sat down next to the snow-dog.
"Thank you so much for trying to help me. It's no fun being on your own all the time. If only I could melt like all my other snow friends," said the snow-dog.
"We like helping you. In fact you've been the best thing about this whole holiday. Even better than playing football!" grinned Tommy.
"You're very nice," said the snow-dog.
"Yeah, and you're cool," laughed Tommy.

It didn't take long for Billy to return with the skateboard and once again the two boys set off for town, pushing the little snow-dog. They did get some strange looks as they walked, some people even asked what was under the coat, but the boys just smiled and said

nothing. They walked past the school, the newsagents, the hairdressers, the post-office and the Beauty Salon and stopped on a corner by the supermarket.
"Are we going in there?" asked Billy pointing at the supermarket.
"No we're going to stay right here!" answered Tommy smiling.
"Here? In the street? Well what good is that?" asked Billy.
"Look down," said Tommy. Billy looked down.
"Yeah...and?"
"Look down, under the snow-dog. What do you see?" asked Tommy.
"Metal with holes in it, so what?" said Billy confused.
"And what is coming out of the holes in the metal?" asked Tommy grinning from ear to ear.
"Air?" replied Billy, still very confused.
"What sort of air?" asked Tommy again his eyes twinkling.
"Oxygen!" replied Billy, definitely very puzzled.
"No don't be daft, bend down and touch the air coming out of those holes!" said Tommy.

Billy bent down and touched the air coming out of the metal holes.
"Owww it's hot!" said Billy pulling his hand away.
"Exactly!" grinned Tommy.
"Ohhhh...I get it!" smiled Billy.

The boys were standing outside the baker's shop. Underneath the baker's there were huge ovens which baked the bread. The hot air coming from the ovens came up through the floor, through metal holes and out into the street.

When Tommy's mum had told him about the fresh bread this morning, he'd thought about the baker's ovens. At first he thought about putting the snow-dog inside one of the baker's ovens, but they'd tried going in shops before and got in a lot of trouble. Then Tommy had remembered the hot air coming out into the street and his plan had come to him in a flash. They couldn't get in trouble this time because they weren't even inside a shop; they were just standing in the street!

"Very clever Tommy, you can't get in trouble for standing outside a shop," laughed Billy.
"No, not even us!" smiled Tommy.
The two boys explained the plan to the snow-dog, who agreed it sounded very clever. Then they took the snow-dog off the skateboard and put him onto the hot metal. Billy took his coat off snow-dog because he didn't want it to get wet when their little friend melted and the boys sat down to watch. Tommy checked his

watch after 5 minutes, nothing had happened so far but they could stay here as long as they wanted.

"Billy I'm just going to the supermarket over there to get a drink, it's hot just watching. Do you want one?" asked Tommy.

"Yeah, something orange," said Billy.

"I'll be five minutes, just stay here and watch, OK?" asked Tommy.

"Yeah OK!" replied Billy, far more interested in the football magazine he was reading. Tommy crossed the road and went into the supermarket. Billy put on his headphones and listened to his favourite music, his head still stuck in his magazine.

If Billy had been paying attention he would have looked up and seen a little girl and her mum walking past the baker's. He would have seen the little girl point at the snow-dog and ask her mum what was happening. If Billy had been paying attention he would have seen the businessman stop and ask the lady what they were looking at. He would have heard two children stop their bikes and join the man, the lady and the little girl outside the baker's. If he'd been paying attention he would have noticed a small crowd of people in the street staring at the small snow-dog. But Billy was listening to music and reading a magazine. He was not paying attention and he did not see the crowd of people outside the baker's.

However, inside Giuseppe the baker had noticed a large crowd growing outside his shop. Giuseppe was Italian, very proud of his work but known to be a little hot-tempered.
"Hey Luigi! Whatsa going on outside my shop?" asked Giuseppe in a thick Italian accent.

"Don'ta know boss!" answered Luigi his assistant.
"Whyssa all the peeple in front of my door?" asked Luigi.
"Don'ta know boss!" answered Luigi again.
"Why hasa nobody come in and buy my bread in the last tenna minuto?" asked Giuseppe.
"Don'ta know boss!" answered Luigi again.

"I'll tell you why Luigi, because the peeple are too busy looking to be buying, thatsa why!" said Giuseppe crossly.
"Yessa boss!" replied Luigi.
"Well I'm gonna go outta there and getta rid of whoever is stopping my customers!" barked Giuseppe and he rolled up his sleeves and marched out of the shop.

    The supermarket was very busy so it took Tommy more than five minutes to buy a drink. But when he came out of the supermarket he couldn't believe what he saw. Outside the baker's was a huge crowd of people standing and staring. Tommy quickly realized that they could only be staring at one thing…the snow-dog. He hurried over to the bakers and managed to squeeze his way through the crowds. Then what he saw was even more surprising. Poor Billy was sat on the floor with his magazine and his headphones still on while a huge man with a black moustache stood over him poking him with a long breadstick! Tommy rushed to help Billy.

"Whatta ya thinka you doing?" shouted the baker at Billy.

"Err...what?" replied Billy, who still couldn't hear anything.

"Whatta ya thinka you doing?" the baker shouted again, but louder.

"Err...what?" said Billy, reaching up to remove his headphones.

"WHATTA YA THINKA YOU DOING?!!" screamed the baker, almost deafening poor Billy.

Tommy pushed his way to the front and stood between Billy and the furious baker.

"Sorry. Sometimes my friend can be a little slow to understand things," smiled Tommy, trying to calm the furious baker down. He now looked like the top of his head may totally blow off like the famous Italian volcano Vesuvius.

"Nobody coming inna my shop. Everybody looking at your doogy!" Giuseppe the baker spluttered.

"Our doogy?" replied Tommy confused.

"Yes youra doogy!" repeated Giuseppe.

"Our doogy?" Tommy questioned again, anxious not to anger the large baker.

"Yessa your doogy, there!" said Giuseppe crossly.
"Oh our dog, yeah we were just trying to melt it!" replied Tommy.
"No...no...no...NO! No melta the doogy. If it melt, it fall on my ovens and boomba...they blow up!!" shouted Giuseppe.
"Oh, I'm sorry," said Tommy. "We'll go then."
"Yes you better *muovere*!"
"Muvo what o?" asked Billy.
"Muovere...MOVE!" the baker bellowed, waving his breadstick viciously.

Tommy grabbed Billy; they put the snow-dog back on the skateboard and ran away as fast as they could. The furious baker was still waving his breadstick at them.

When they got back to the meadow they sat down, tired and disappointed.
"I'm sorry little guy," Tommy said patting the little white dog on the head. "I guess that didn't work either?"
"Don't worry," said the snow-dog dejectedly. "I guess I'll just never melt. I just wish it wasn't so lonely."
Tommy felt so sorry for the snow-dog. He knew that the poor little dog was miserable but he also knew time was running out. Even Billy seemed to have no new ideas.
"Look, tomorrow is our last day before we go back to school. We'll think of something tomorrow," Tommy said trying to cheer up their little friend.

They left the snow-dog in the meadow and trudged home.
"Can't believe we'll be back in old Walrus-face's class again soon," moaned Billy.
"Look on the bright-side mate. At least old Jeffries isn't as scary as that Italian baker."
"Yeah, or my Aunt Judy," grinned Billy.
"See ya tomorrow mate."

Tommy went straight up into his bedroom and stared out the window. His plan had been even worse than Billy's. They had one day left before they went back to school. How were they ever going to melt snow-dog now?

6. Snow-Dog's too cool!

The next morning, Tommy didn't wake up quite so excited. None of their ideas to help the snow-dog had worked so far. The sun hadn't melted him. The radiator and hairdryer hadn't melted him. The tanning machine hadn't melted him. Even the hot air at the baker's hadn't melted him. All that had happened was that he and Billy had got in trouble. What were they going to do? He yawned, rubbed his eyes and walked over to his calendar. He picked up the pen and drew a line through Sunday. The next day was Monday and it had 'Back to School' written on it. Tommy sighed and went back to bed. He just couldn't think of another way to melt the snow-dog. Tommy's mum knocked on the door and came in.

"Morning sleepy," she said. "Morning mum," replied Tommy miserably, pulling the covers back over his head.

"I thought you'd be in a bad mood today. No football always puts you in a mood," his mum said smiling.
"What do you mean no football?" asked Tommy from underneath the covers.
"Well, haven't you looked out the window? It snowed all night last night. Everything's covered in snow," said mum.
"Oh," said Tommy, not really interested in the snow.
But as Tommy thought about the snow an idea popped into his head. And not an idea like the others, this was a great idea. Tommy threw off the covers, leapt out of bed and pulled back the curtains.

"Mum you're right. It's been snowing. Fantastic!" he laughed as he quickly pulled on some clothes over his pyjamas.
"What do you mean fantastic? You hate snow, don't you?" asked his mum very confused.
"Not today mum…not today. Don't worry about it mum, you're the best!" smiled Tommy as he kissed his mum and bounded down the stairs.
"What about your breakfast?" shouted his mum.

But Tommy was gone already racing across the meadow. Tommy's mum shook her head.
"I will *never* understand ten year old boys!" she said.

Billy was just as fed up as Tommy. He'd been sitting at the breakfast table trying to think of a way to melt the snow-dog and hadn't come up with anything. He'd been sitting there nearly an hour and his cereal had all gone soggy. He was pushing the soggy cereal round the bowl when Tommy burst in.
"Billy, Billy, it's snowing!" said an excited Tommy.
"Yeah, so what?" replied a miserable Billy.
"Well it's given me an idea!" said Tommy grinning.
"No Tommy. No more ideas. I'm fed up with getting in trouble. I nearly got battered by a breadstick yesterday!" said Billy sulking.
"I know, I know. But this idea is different, and we won't get into trouble!" smiled Tommy.
"You promise?" asked Billy.

"I promise!" laughed Tommy.
"Alright, but how are we going to melt him?" asked Billy.
"You'll see. Now come on let's go!" said Tommy grabbing Billy's arm.
"To the meadow?" asked Billy.
"No...somewhere else!" said Tommy with a glint in his eye.

Tommy raced along with Billy struggling to keep up with him. They ran down the street and Tommy skidded to a halt outside their school.
"This is it!" smiled Tommy.
"No it isn't. This is school. We don't have to be here until tomorrow. Come on let's go, I don't want to spend the last day of the holidays at school!" said Billy, turning to go back.
"No Billy come on, we have to go to the playground," said Tommy grabbing hold of his coat.
"The gate's locked and you promised me we wouldn't get in trouble," said Billy.
"We won't. Old Smithy the caretaker is still on holiday. No-one comes back until tomorrow. Now help me over the gate," said Tommy.

"Alright, alright," said Billy grumbling. "I can't see how this is going to help the snow-dog melt!"
"You'll see," laughed Tommy as Billy helped him over the gate.
Tommy turned around and helped pull Billy up and over the gate. Then they both landed in the playground, which was covered in soft white snow.
"Perfect!" said Tommy smiling.
'Never heard you call school that before," said a puzzled Billy.
"Not the school, the playground. It's perfect!" smiled Tommy.
"I think you've gone crazy!" said Billy looking at his friend.
"You'll see!" laughed Tommy. "You'll see!"

   Three hours later the boys climbed back over the school fence. Billy's smile was now as big as Tommy's and they ran as fast as they could towards the meadow. When they got there the snow-dog was just where they'd left him. Billy carried on running to his house and Tommy sat down and patted the little snow-dog on the head.

"Hello Tommy," said the snow-dog sadly.
"Hello little snow-dog," smiled Tommy.
"It's snowing again. I'll never melt now," said snow-dog miserably.
"Don't worry. I've had another idea!" said Tommy.
"Will it help me melt?" asked the snow-dog.
"Wait and see," smiled Tommy. "Wait and see!"

Billy returned with his sled and a big smile on his face. The two boys gently picked up the little snow-dog and put him on the sled. Then they pulled him across the meadow and stopped outside their school. Billy helped Tommy climb over the school gate and then Tommy pulled Billy up and over. The snow-dog was just small enough to squeeze through the gap in the bars of the fence. The boys turned the sled on its side, squeezed it through the bars, put the snow-dog back on it and pulled him into the playground.
"And this, snow-dog, is our playground," smiled Billy.
When snow dog looked at the playground he couldn't believe what he saw. The

playground was covered with snowmen, snow-women, snow-children, snow-dogs and even snow-cats.

"We thought because you were so lonely we'd build you lots of friends to keep you company," said Tommy.

"It was Tommy's idea. If we can't melt you, we'll just make sure you'll never get lonely again!" said Billy happily.

"Oh thank you, thank you," said the snow-dog his eyes shining with happiness.

"Come on snow-dog, let's go for a spin and meet some of your new friends," laughed Tommy.

Tommy and Billy happily pulled snow-dog around and around the playground. As they weaved in and out of all the snow statues they'd built the little snow-dog barked happily. After a while the two boys sat down, red in the face, tired but still smiling happily.

"This, snow-dog is your new home. You can live here on the wall in our school playground and you'll never be lonely again," said Billy.
But the little snow-dog looked sad again.
"What is it snow-dog? What's the matter?" asked Tommy.
"This is the best thing anyone has ever done for me. But as soon as it stops snowing all my new friends will melt. I won't melt and then I'll be all on my own again!" sniffed the little snow-dog unhappily.
Billy and Tommy smiled at the snow-dog and patted him on his head.

"No you won't, snow-dog. Don't you see? There are over three hundred children who go to this school everyday. You'll have over three hundred friends everyday!" smiled Billy.
"Yes, and we'll see you everyday. You won't need snow-friends, you've got us!" said Tommy grinning at the little snow-dog.
The snow-dog looked at Billy and Tommy's happy faces. Then his orange

peel mouth curled into a huge smile and he let out some happy little barks.
"Oh thank you Tommy, thank you Billy. You're the best friends a snow-dog could ever have. Can I ask you one more favour?" asked the snow-dog.
"Sure!" said the two boys together.
"Can you pull me around the playground again? That was cool!" smiled the snow-dog.
"Yeah, let's go!" shouted Tommy grabbing hold of the ropes on the sled. As snow-dog barked happily Billy looked at Tommy.
"Snow-dog's cool!" Billy laughed.
"No...you mean snow-dog is **too** cool!" said Tommy.

"Oh, I get it!" laughed Billy. "You mean too cool to melt!"

"Exactly, Snow-Dog's **too** cool!" laughed Tommy.

THE END

...but Tommy and Billy will return in...

.... Tommy Tomkins and the Curse of the Thought Bubble.

About the Author

Jon Bridgeman started writing for children in 2001. He has written many short stories, poems and is still writing his 'masterpiece' a fantasy novel for children. His first published work was 'The Gingerbread Rapper'. He hopes that his second book 'Tommy Tomkins and the Snowdog' will be followed by many more. Jon's ideas and inspiration come from years spent as a classroom teacher and reading stories to children. 'If it makes me laugh...it normally makes them giggle too!'

About the Illustrator

Rachel Cooper is a busy artist, teacher and mum! She began drawing children's books at university and continued drawing when she began teaching. Stranded on a Caribbean island in 2003 with no books to teach with she began drawing and making her own books. She is delighted that years of practice have finally seen her drawings in print.

Find out more about author and illustrator at:
www.montaguepublishing.co.uk